Which Is Longest?

A CRABTREE SEEDLINGS BOOK

Alan Walker

CRABTREE
PUBLISHING COMPANY
WWW.CRABTREEBOOKS.COM

What is long?

What is short?

The giraffe has
long legs.

The dog has short legs.

The boy has short hair.

The girl has long hair.

This car is long.

This car is short.

This rope is long.

This rope is short.

This sandwich is long.

This sandwich is short.

13

Which is longest?

We pack for long trips.

We also take short trips.

Which trip is long?

Which trip is short?

Which is longest?

School-to-Home Support for Caregivers and Teachers

Crabtree Seedlings books help children grow by letting them practice reading. Here are a few guiding questions to help the reader with building his or her comprehension skills. Possible answers are included.

Before Reading

- What do I think this book is about? I think this book is about things that are long and short. I think it will help us see which things are longer than others.

- What do I want to learn about this topic? I want to learn how to measure how long an object is.

During Reading

- I wonder why... I wonder why giraffes have long legs and necks.

- What have I learned so far? I have learned that I can line objects up to tell which one is the longest.

After Reading

- What details did I learn about this topic? I learned that people take long and short trips. People travel farther on long trips. They bring suitcases.

- Write down unfamiliar words and ask questions to help understand their meaning. I see the word **pack** on page 16. The picture shows a suitcase. People fill suitcases with things they want to take with them on trips. Does pack mean to fill a suitcase?

Library and Archives Canada Cataloging-in-Publication Data

Title: Which is longest? / Alan Walker.
Names: Walker, Alan, 1963- author.
Description: Series statement: Early learning concepts | "A Crabtree seedlings book". | Previously
    published in electronic format by Blue Door Education in 2020.
Identifiers: Canadiana 20200385607 | ISBN 9781427128508 (hardcover) | ISBN 9781427128584 (softcover)
Subjects: LCSH: Length measurement—Juvenile literature.
Classification: LCC QC102 .W35 2021 | DDC j530.8—dc23

Library of Congress Cataloging-in-Publication Data

Names: Walker, Alan, 1963- author.
Title: Which is longest? / Alan Walker.
Description: New York : Crabtree Publishing, 2021. | Series: Early learning concepts : a Crabtree seedlings book
Identifiers: LCCN 2020049642 | ISBN 9781427128508 (hardcover) | ISBN 9781427128584 (paperback)
Subjects: LCSH: Length measurement--Juvenile literature. | Mathematics--Juvenile literature. | English language--Comparison--Juvenile literature.
Classification: LCC QC102 .W34 2021 | DDC 530.8--dc23
LC record available at https://lccn.loc.gov/2020049642

Crabtree Publishing Company

www.crabtreebooks.com   1-800-387-7650

e-book ISBN 978-1-947632-74-5
Print book version produced jointly with Crabtree Publishing Company NY, USA

Written by Alan Walker
Production coordinator and Prepress technician: Amy Salter
Print coordinator: Katherine Berti

Printed in the USA/012021/CG20201102

Photo credits: istock.com, Shutterstock.com, Cover; ©istock.com/Lyubov Kobyakova. Pg2/3; ©istock.com/WestLight. Pg4/5; ©istock.com/Alex Potemkin, ©istock.com/Tijana87. Pg6/7; ©istock.com/Wavebreakmedia, ©istock.com/Koraysa. Pg8/9; ©istock.com/nycshooter. Pg10/11; ©istock.com/Zoran Kolundzija, Zocha_K. Pg12/13; ©istock.com/jabiru, ©istock.com/Bestfotostudio. Pg14/15; ©istock.com/vitsirisukodom. Pg16/17; ©istock.com/PicturePartners. Pg16/17; ©istock.com/monticelllo, ©istock.com/Vera_Petrunina   Pg18/19; ©istock.com/alexandr_1958. Pg20/21; ©istock.com/coffeee-in. Pg22/23; ©istock.com/Cjoakimbkk.

Published in Canada	Published in the United States	Published in the United Kingdom	Published in Australia
Crabtree Publishing	Crabtree Publishing	Crabtree Publishing	Crabtree Publishing
616 Welland Ave.	347 Fifth Ave	Maritime House	Unit 3 – 5
St. Catharines, ON	Suite 1402-145	Basin Road North, Hove	Currumbin Court
L2M 5V6	New York, NY 10016	BN41 1WR	Capalaba QLD 4157